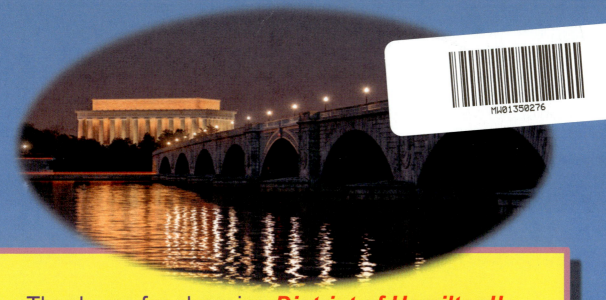

Thank you for choosing *District of Hamilton!!*

Learning how to rap all the words in *Hamilton: The Musical* made us want to learn more about the people we were singing about.

Although Hamilton himself didn't spend much time in **Washington, DC**, there are many, many references to him in our public buildings and parks. Also, many of our founding fathers (and founding mothers like Martha Washington and Eliza) – people Hamilton called colleagues, friends, and enemies, lived and worked here and left their marks.

We hope you'll have fun following the path of Hamilton in DC and finding the clues to solve the **Treasure Hunt**. Most of these sites are free!

We started this project in January 2018 and finished in May 2018, just in time for *Hamilton: The Musical* to come to the Kennedy Center! We have donated copies to our local library. You can buy extra copies on **Amazon.com**. **#DistrictOfHamilton**

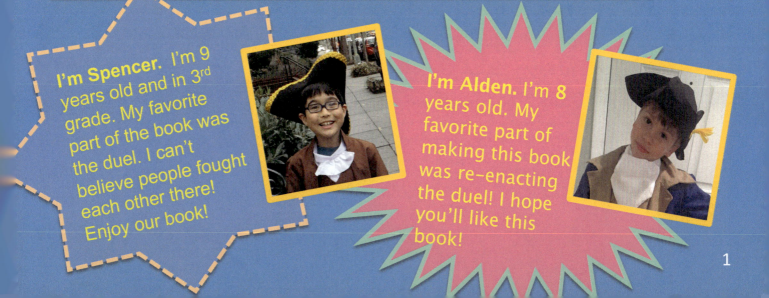

I'm Spencer. I'm 9 years old and in 3rd grade. My favorite part of the book was the duel. I can't believe people fought each other there! Enjoy our book!

I'm Alden. I'm 8 years old. My favorite part of making this book was re-enacting the duel! I hope you'll like this book!

Table of Contents

1. The National Archives……5
2. The Treasury Department….9
3. Bureau of Engraving and Printing…11
4. Lafayette Square……13
5. White House Visitor's Center……14
6. The Washington Monument……15
7. The Jefferson Memorial……16
8. Natl. Museum of American History…18
9. Capitol Building……21
10. The Library of Congress……24
11. National Portrait Gallery……26
12. State Department……27
13. Hamilton Memorial……28
14. The Society of the Cincinnati…29
15. Eliza's Home and Church……31
16. Dueling Grounds……35
17. Mount Vernon……36
18. Monticello……40
19. The Battlefield at Yorktown….44
20. American Revolution Museum at Yorktown……45
21. Free Donuts and Ice Cream! ……47-48

Monticello picture ©Thomas Jefferson Foundation at Monticello

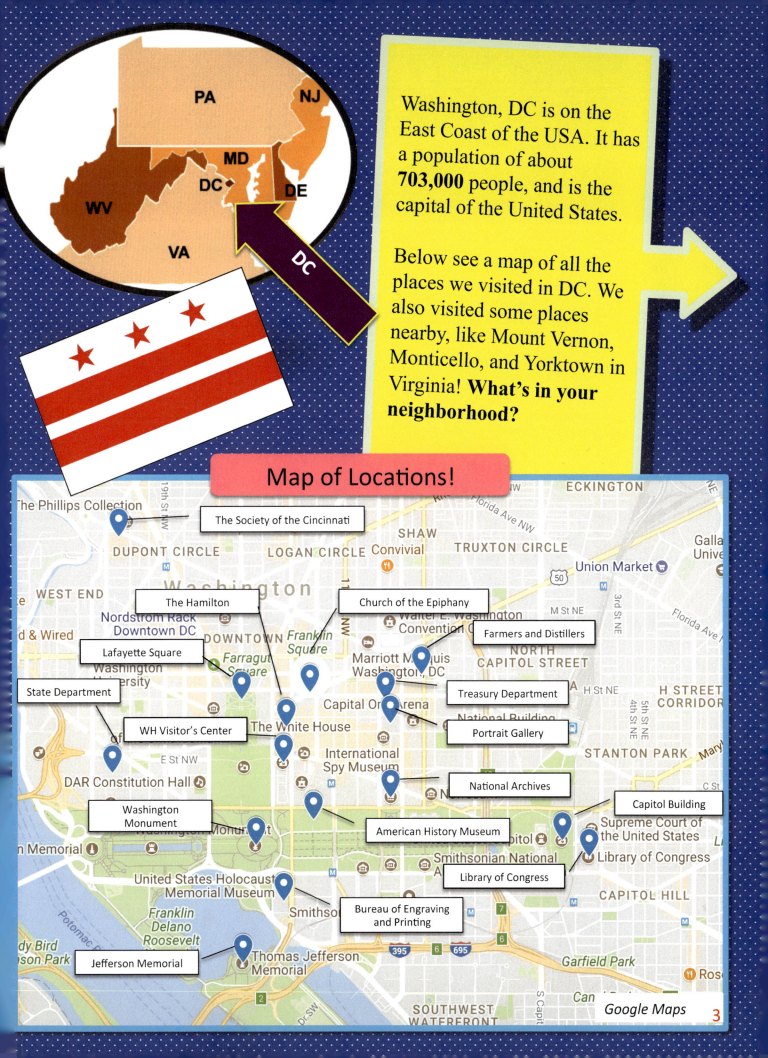

Washington, DC is on the East Coast of the USA. It has a population of about **703,000** people, and is the capital of the United States.

Below see a map of all the places we visited in DC. We also visited some places nearby, like Mount Vernon, Monticello, and Yorktown in Virginia! **What's in your neighborhood?**

Map of Locations!

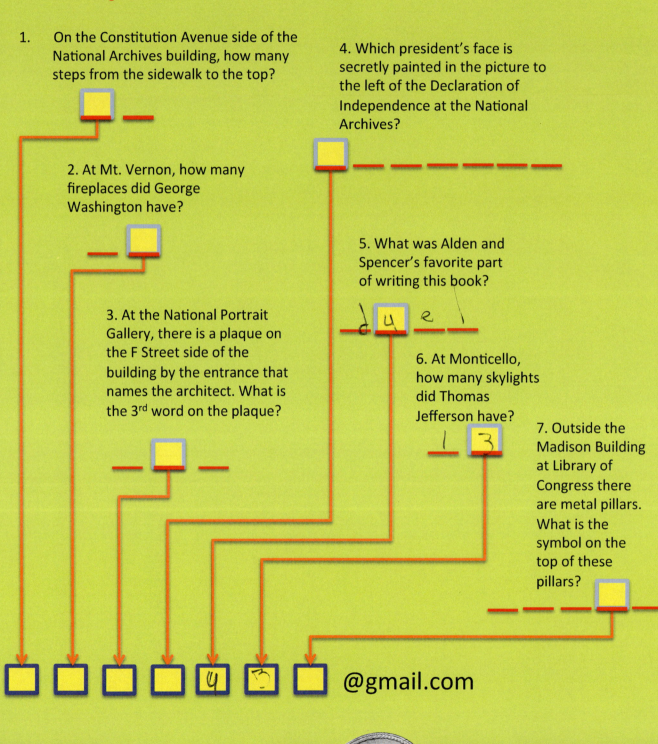

This book is a Treasure Hunt too!

Visit some of the places included in this book. Answer the questions below to figure out the **secret** email address. Ask your parent to send a message to the email address and receive a **surprise!**

1. On the Constitution Avenue side of the National Archives building, how many steps from the sidewalk to the top? ___

2. At Mt. Vernon, how many fireplaces did George Washington have? ___

3. At the National Portrait Gallery, there is a plaque on the F Street side of the building by the entrance that names the architect. What is the 3rd word on the plaque? ___

4. Which president's face is secretly painted in the picture to the left of the Declaration of Independence at the National Archives? ___ ___ ___ ___ ___ ___

5. What was Alden and Spencer's favorite part of writing this book? d u e l

6. At Monticello, how many skylights did Thomas Jefferson have? 1 3

7. Outside the Madison Building at Library of Congress there are metal pillars. What is the symbol on the top of these pillars? ___ ___ ___ ___

___ ___ ___ ___ 4 3 ___ @gmail.com

Treasury Department
799 9th Street, NW

What the Treasury Building looked like when it was first built in 1800.

The Treasury Building was the first completed government building when the capitol was moved to DC in **1800**. It has been almost destroyed by fire three times – being rebuilt every time! Alexander Hamilton was the first Secretary of the Treasury but he never worked in this building. **Albert Gallatin**, in the statue to the left, was the Secretary of the Treasury under Presidents Jefferson and Madison.

Alex says: Who is this dude? Everyone probably thinks HE's the first Treasury Secretary.

Spencer says: Alex was right. That was Albert Gallatin, not Hamilton. Hamilton's statue is on the other side of the building.

Hamilton!

White House Visitor's Center
1450 Pennsylvania Ave., NW

The White House Visitor's Center is a great place to learn about what life is like for our presidents!

Alex says: All the presidents have good tchotchkes here – except ME, because I was never president. Seriously lame. I mean, who wants a John Adams ornament anyway?

Fun fact: President James A. Garfield's favorite food was squirrel soup!

Fun fact: President Reagan really loved jelly beans!

14

Washington Monument
14th and Connecticut, NW

The Washington Monument is the world's tallest stone structure and the tallest obelisk, at **555** feet tall. Eliza Hamilton helped raise funds to build the monument in honor of George Washington's contribution to our country. Construction began in **1848**, and stopped in 1854 from lack of funds and the intervention of the Civil War. It was finally completed in 1884. Obelisks, four sided pillars that end in a pyramid shape, were used by the ancient Egyptians, Greeks, and Romans.

Alex says: This is the newspaper announcement of a ball my darling Eliza held in DC to raise funds for the monument!

Fun fact: If you look about halfway up the monument, you'll see where the break was!

Halfway point

Jefferson Memorial
701 East Basin Drive, SW

Alex says: Ugh. Of course he got a monument and I didn't. Prima donna.

Alden says: Pillars were a common thing to have on buildings from this time.

The Jefferson Memorial was completed in 1943, but the statue of Jefferson inside wasn't added until 4 years later. There are **44** steps leading up to this neo-classical building.

WE HOLD THESE TRUTHS TO BE SELF-EVIDENT: THAT ALL MEN ARE CREATED EQUAL, THAT THEY ARE ENDOWED BY THEIR CREATOR WITH CERTAIN INALIENABLE RIGHTS, AMONG THESE ARE LIFE, LIBERTY AND THE PURSUIT OF HAPPINESS, THAT TO SECURE THESE RIGHTS GOVERNMENTS ARE INSTITUTED AMONG MEN. WE... SOLEMNLY PUBLISH AND DECLARE, THAT THESE COLONIES ARE AND OF RIGHT OUGHT TO BE FREE AND INDEPENDENT STATES...AND FOR THE SUPPORT OF THIS DECLARATION, WITH A FIRM RELIANCE ON THE PROTECTION OF DIVINE PROVIDENCE, WE MUTUALLY PLEDGE OUR LIVES, OUR FORTUNES AND OUR SACRED HONOUR.

Alex says: **President Franklin Delano Roosevelt** was the one who wanted to build this memorial – you can see it from the back porch of the White House! FDR actually laid the cornerstone. There was a group of women who didn't want it to be built because it destroyed their favorite beach, so they tied themselves to trees on the site. The siege ended when they had to take a bathroom break!

Fun fact: The shape of the domed ceiling is the same as the one at Jefferson's home in Monticello.

Burr - the guy who killed me!

When Burr was Vice President under Jefferson, he was also the President of the Senate. That's why there is a bust of Burr in the Senate Gallery.

Alex says: Excellent name, if I do say so myself!

Each state gets to put a statue of a famous citizen from that state in the Capitol rotunda.

Hamilton quote!

Library of Congress
101 Independence Avenue, SE

The Library of Congress is the research library for Congress, and basically the national library of the United States. It houses many original manuscripts, including the Federalist Papers and drafts of Washington's speeches

Fun fact: There is an underground tunnel between the Capitol and the Library of Congress main building!

The Federalist Papers are here!

Alden says: The Federalist Papers are locked up because someone might steal them.

There are dozens of these posts outside the **Library of Congress**. Notice that the seal on them changes depending on what building you are near!

The Hamilton papers have been digitized, so they are only available for view online: https://www.loc.gov/collections/alexander-hamilton-papers/about-this-collection/ but the originals (including the Federalist Papers) are kept at the Library of Congress Madison Building.

Alex says: Notes on my plan for a new government at the Federal Convention.

Alex says: Madison got this whole building named after him!

Alex says: Letter I wrote to **Eliza**

25

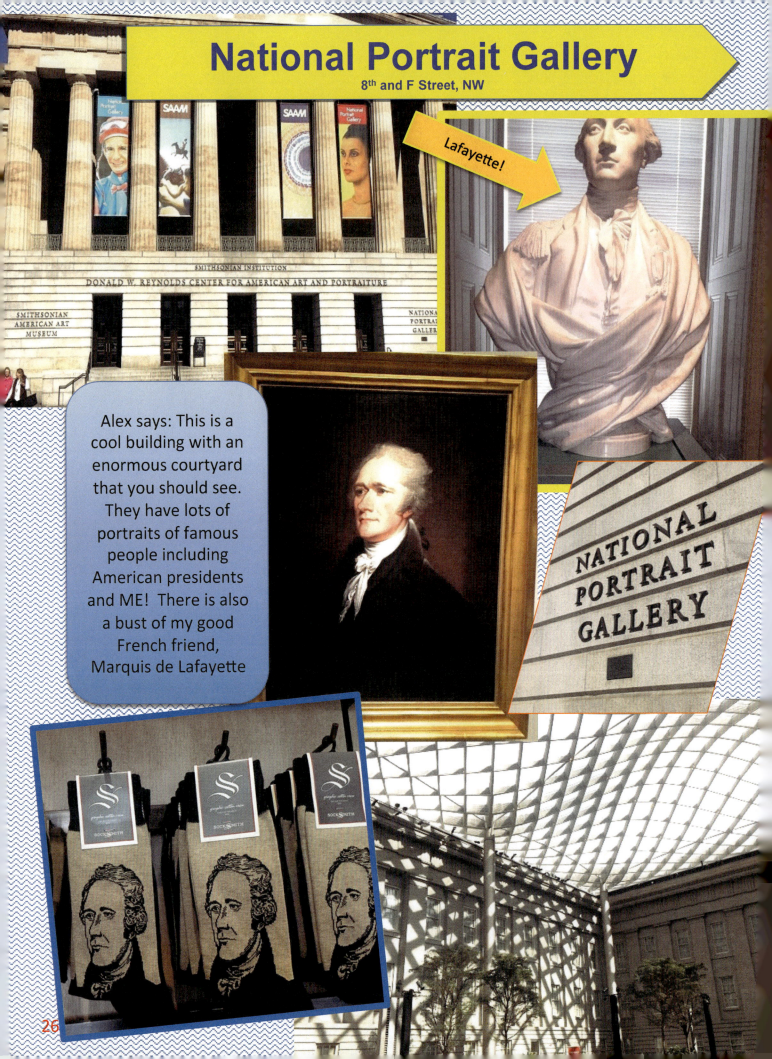

State Department
2201 C Street, NW

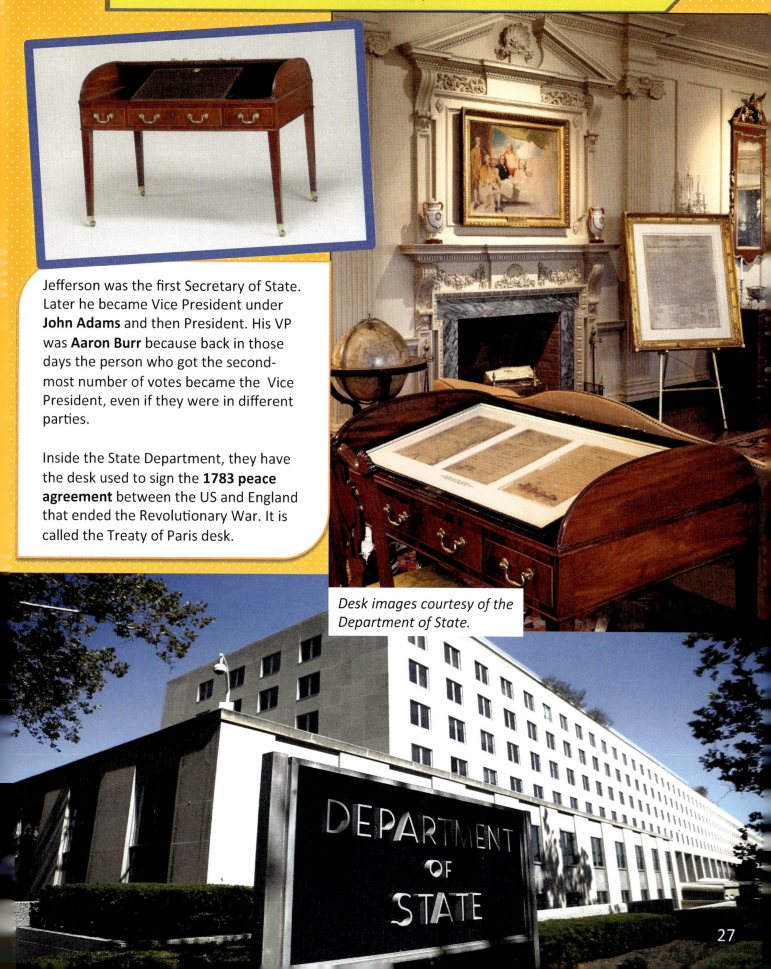

Jefferson was the first Secretary of State. Later he became Vice President under **John Adams** and then President. His VP was **Aaron Burr** because back in those days the person who got the second-most number of votes became the Vice President, even if they were in different parties.

Inside the State Department, they have the desk used to sign the **1783 peace agreement** between the US and England that ended the Revolutionary War. It is called the Treaty of Paris desk.

Desk images courtesy of the Department of State.

27

> **Hamilton Memorial in DC**

Zip. Nothing.

Nada.

No memorial for me.

The Society of the Cincinnati
2118 Massachusetts Avenue, NW

Spencer says: This is a real cannon. I don't know how they carried it inside.

Alex says: After we won the Revolutionary War against the British, Continental Army officers formed a group to remember our friends who died fighting for independence. We named it after the ancient Roman military hero **Lucius Cincinnatus** who defended his land from foreign invaders but refused any reward for his service, just like my friend **George Washington**. In fact, General Washington became the first President General of the **Society of the Cincinnati** and, of course, I became the second President General. The society also helped Revolutionary War widows and orphans.

Alex says: The headquarters of the Society is in **Anderson House**. You can see a painting of me here and learn more about the American Revolution. They also have a **Revolutionary War Camp** in the summer for kids 8-11 years old where they practice writing with quills, cooking with old recipes and soldier drills.

Alex says: What a handsome devil!

Alden says: This is a weird flag. I didn't know what flag it was.

Fun fact: Anderson House has **90** rooms.

30

Eliza Hamilton's Home
1300 Block of H Street, NW

Alex: In **1848**, my dear Eliza moved to Washington when she was 91. She lived with my daughter **Eliza Hamilton Holly** who was also a widow. They lived in a townhouse close to the White House. Eliza spent hours sitting by the window, knitting or making mats.

Many people including Presidents would visit her to learn about George Washington, me and the Revolutionary War.

Eliza rented a townhouse on **H Street, NW between 13th and 14th Streets**, from Mrs. Beverly Kennon (aka Britannia Kennon, the great-granddaughter of Martha Washington!) **General Winfield Scott** was her neighbor. The original buildings are gone, but above is a photo of the block in 1900. Below is the block today.

Atlantic Monthly, Volume LXXVIII, Houghton Mifflin Co., 1896.
Chernow, Ron, *Alexander Hamilton*, Penguin Books, 2004.
Gouverneur, Marian Campbell, *As I Remember: Recollections of American Society During the Nineteenth Century*, D. Appleton & Co., 1911.
Photos courtesy of Library of Congress

Eliza Hamilton's Church
1317 G Street, NW

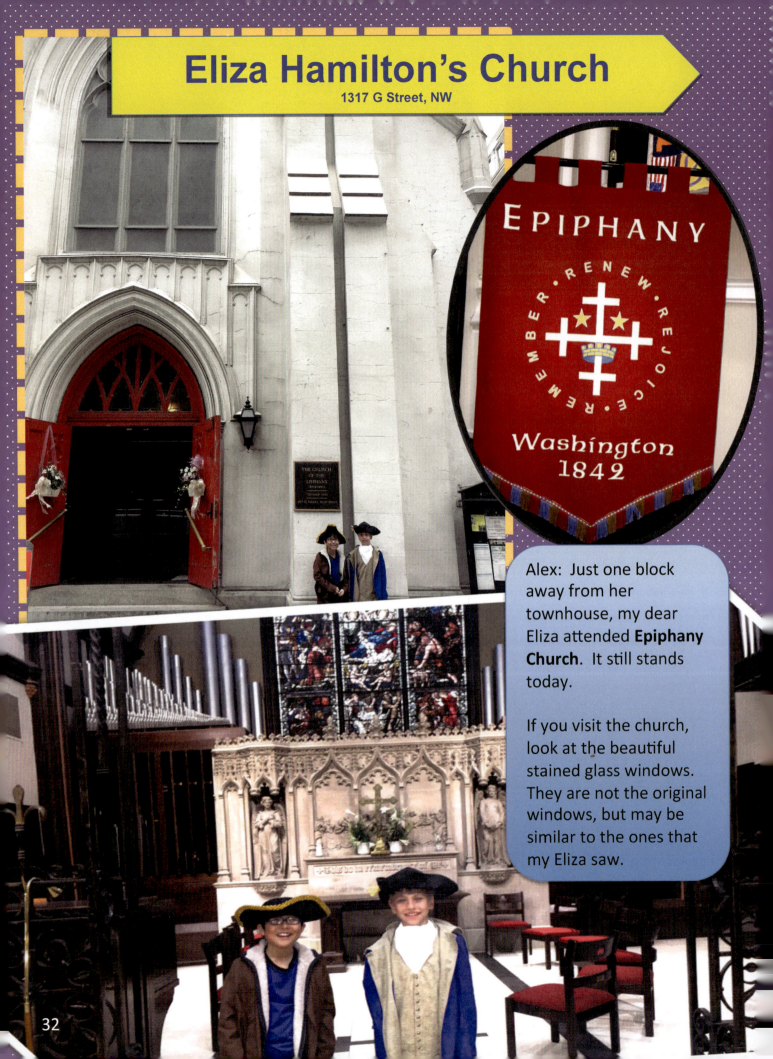

Alex: Just one block away from her townhouse, my dear Eliza attended **Epiphany Church**. It still stands today.

If you visit the church, look at the beautiful stained glass windows. They are not the original windows, but may be similar to the ones that my Eliza saw.

The minister's daughter remembered, "**Mrs. Hamilton's** stately little figure, slowly walking up the aisle of the Church, leaning upon her daughter's arm, dressed, as she always was in silk stockings and black satin slippers, no matter what the weather, a rather short black crepe de chine skirt, and a shawl of finest texture with deep fringe, and a poke bonnet which almost concealed her face. With great dignity **Mrs. Hamilton** entered her pew, which was immediately under the pulpit, where she quietly seated herself. Then, adjusting her ear trumpet, she turned her face toward my Father, and listened motionless to his sermon."

Weir, Mary French, *Rememberances: Biography of Clara Miller-French*, 1920.

Spencer says: This organ had many more keys than my piano at home. But we were not allowed to play it.

Alex: This is what they wrote about Eliza when she died at age **97** in Washington in **1854**. They sent her body by train from Washington to New York to be buried at **Trinity Church**.

"Her benevolence was most exemplary, and one of the finest manifestations of it was her habit, to within a few months of her death, of making occasional visits to all the schools of the city, and she never did so without imparting some moral lesson which showed how deep an interest she took in the welfare of the country which her husband had contributed so largely to make free and independent."

EVENING STAR.
LOCAL INTELLIGENCE.

WASHINGTON.
"Liberty and Union, now and forever, one and inseparable."
SATURDAY, NOVEMBER 21, 185—

Mrs. ELIZABETH HAMILTON, the venerable universally respected relict of ALEXANDER HAMILTON, closed her earthly career at her residence in this city on Thursday morning, the 9th inst., — four o'clock.

She was the second daughter of the distinguished General PHILIP S. SCHUYLER, of Albany, — born on the 9th day of August, 1757. S— married to ALEXANDER HAMILTON, then one — Aids of General WASHINGTON with the — Lieutenant Colonel, on the 9th of December — there being not quite a year's difference i— ages. They lived together in the enjoy— every blessing that could render wedded life h— nearly twenty-four years, and she surviv— mented and distinguished husband more th— a century. To estimate her character prope— necessary to bear in mind that of the individ— had selected her, from the many who wo— been proud of the distinction of his notice— companion of his life; and that character w— beautifully portrayed by a single touch of the — pencil of Mr. WEBSTER, that we give it as — ing in a few words the judgment of one who— of discrimination was seldom surpassed, Mr. W— speaking of Colonel HAMILTON as a hero— Revolution, a jurist, and statesman, Mr. W— " HAMILTON was placed at the head of the T— Department. He carried on the Governme— ces; he smote the rock of the national re— and abundant streams of revenue gushed — He touched the dead corpse of public cre— it sprang upon its feet. The fabled system of — from the brain of Jove was not more perf— the financial system of the United States— sprang from the conception of ALEXANDE— TON." It was this great man who sou— won ELIZABETH SCHUYLER, and that fact is — to show her worth. But, had she been — than an ordinarily endowed woman, it wou— been impossible to have passed twenty-fou— of happy intercourse with such a husband — having her mind richly stored from the trea— his mighty intellect; and those who knew h— in her declining years will be ready to test— she was a rare example of the wisdom taug— servant experience, and a bright example — womanly graces. Her benevolence was mos— plary, and one of the finest manifestations — her habit, to within a few months of her d— making occasional visits to all the schoo— city, and she never did so without im— some moral lesson which showed how d— interest she took in the welfare of the country — her husband had contributed so largely to m— and independent.

Mrs. HAMILTON lived to the very advan— of ninety-seven years and three months, a— without a struggle, in full communion — Episcopal Church and surrounded by her su— children. Her remains were taken to Ne— for interment.

DEATH OF A DISTINGUISHED LADY.—We have heretofore noticed the dangerous illness of Mrs. Alexander Hamilton, the venerated widow of General Alexander Hamilton, an aid to Gen. Washington in the Revolution, and the first Secretary of the Treasury of the United States. Notwithstanding the most skillful attentions of the attending physician, Dr. Hall, and the assiduous nursing of her affectionate daughter, Mrs. Holley, she expired yesterday morning. Her two sons, James A. and John C. Hamilton, Esq., of New York, were also present at her illness and death. The remains were taken to the depot this morning, and left for New York, accompanied only by the family. Mrs. Hamilton was the daughter of Gen Philip S. Schuyler, of Albany, distinguished in the Revolutionary war. She lived to the very advanced aged of ninety-seven years and three months, and died without a struggle, in full communion with the Episcopal church, and surrounded by her surviving children and a few particular friends.

Courtesy Library of Congress, Chronicling America: Historic American Newspapers site

Dueling Grounds
Arlington, VA and Bladensburg, MD

There are several dueling grounds just outside of DC. One is in **Arlington, Virginia**, and the other is in **Bladensburg, Maryland**. Most duels end with nobody getting hurt. Hamilton had been involved in duel preliminaries six times, and three times had acted as a "second" in a duel. But he had never been in a duel himself until the final fatal duel with Aaron Burr.*

Alex says: If you ever find yourself in a duel, do not throw away your shot!

*Chernow, Ron, *Alexander Hamilton*, Penguin Books, 2004.

Mount Vernon
3200 Mount Vernon Highway, Mount Vernon, VA

Fun fact: Mount Vernon has 21 rooms and 13 fire places. **12 to 15** slaves lived in the house with the family where there was no electricity, no plumbing, and no air conditioning. They used chamber pots!

Mount Vernon is George Washington's home. The original house was built in **1735**, when Washington was only 3. He acquired this mansion in 1754. The grounds include gardens, a farm, slave quarters, and Washington's burial vault. They raise rare breeds of hogs on the farm!

Alden says: This was the smallest mansion I ever saw!

The bed in which George Washington died.

Bedchamber photo courtesy of George Washington's Mount Vernon

Fun fact: Mount Vernon has a weathervane in the shape of a dove, the symbol for peace. Washington had it made and installed while he was presiding over the **Constitutional Convention** in 1787.

Spencer says: Go see the stables for the horses. They were bigger than these slave quarters.

These are the slave quarters. There were **317** slaves at Mount Vernon at the time of George Washington's death. His will required that the ones owned by him be freed upon his wife's death. He was the only slaveholding founding father to free his slaves in his will.

Fun fact: They raise animal breeds on the farm that were popular in the 1700's. Some types of hogs there only exist at Mount Vernon!

George and Martha Washington's tomb

Monticello
931 Thomas Jefferson Parkway, Charlottesville, VA

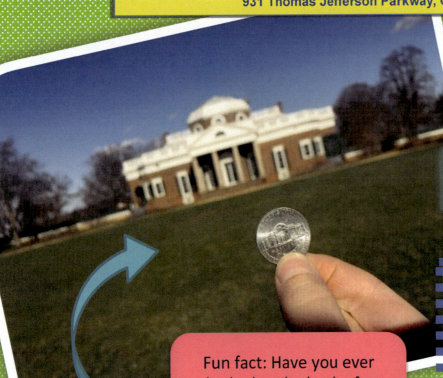

If you visit Monticello in the spring time you'll see a lot of me in all of the nooks and crannies!

Before Jefferson went to Europe

After Jefferson went to Europe

Fun fact: Have you ever looked at the back of a nickel? It's not the White House, it's Monticello!

Alex says: Monticello is Jefferson's home near Charlottesville, Virginia. In one of the main rooms, there are busts of all of the founding fathers, including me!

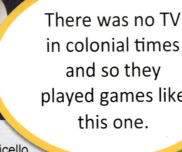

There was no TV in colonial times and so they played games like this one.

©Thomas Jefferson Foundation at Monticello

Thomas Jefferson was buried on the grounds of Monticello, in the family graveyard.

Jefferson died on **July 4, 1826**, 5 hours before John Adams, exactly 50 years after the signing of the Declaration of Independence.

American Revolution Museum at Yorktown

200 Water Street, Yorktown, VA

Nearby is the American Revolution Museum at Yorktown. There is a film that describes the history of the war and how it affected ordinary people. In another theater, they show a panoramic video of the battle with **4-D** action! Outside, there are people in colonial outfits showing what life was like in those days.

Hard Tack

Alden says: The food they ate had to be dried because they had to carry it in their backpacks.

Salt Pork

Spencer says: We learned how Continental Army soldiers loaded and fired flintlock muskets. They were very tricky and don't always work.

Continental Army Encampment

The historical interpreters show live demonstrations of musket firing!

Fun fact: They used muskets, even though they are less accurate than the rifles, because they could be loaded faster and they could be made quickly and cheaply.

The Hamilton
600 14th Street, NW

EAT · DRINK · LISTEN

The Hamilton is a restaurant near the White House that is dedicated to Hamilton and is great for a large crowd. **If you bring in a copy of this book before December 31, 2018, you will receive a free dessert!**

Fun fact: Eliza Hamilton introduced George Washington to ice cream in **1789**.

Acknowledgements

Thank you to the many people and institutions in **DC** and beyond who spared time to show us the sights, sounds, and documents of the Founding Fathers and the Revolutionary War period. They make history come alive!

- Miriam Kleiman and James Pritchett, National Archives
- Dawn Bonner, Mount Vernon
- Mia Magruder and Tasha Stanton, Monticello
- Kym Hall, Yorktown Battlefield
- Homer Lanier, Susan Bak, and Tracy Perkins, American Revolution Museum at Yorktown
- Kevin Brown, Bureau of Engraving and Printing, Treasury Department
- Tripp Jones and Arrien Davison, Church of the Epiphany
- Jessica Smith, Washington Historical Society
- Wendy Kail, Tudor Place Historic House and Garden
- Megan Sheils, Bunche Library, State Department
- Gayle Osterberg, Library of Congress
- Porter Wilkinson, Smithsonian Institution
- National Museum of American History
- Na Lee, Founding Farmers
- Maureen Hirsch, Clyde's Restaurant Group
- Glenn Hennessey, The Society of the Cincinnati
- Of course Lin-Manuel Miranda and Ron Chernow too!

If you are interested in researching more, some great internet resources are:

- **Library of Congress, Chronicling America:** Historic American Newspapers site, https://chroniclingamerica.loc.gov/
- **National Archives, Founders Online:** https://founders.archives.gov/
- **Hamilton Schuyler Compendium:** http://hamiltonschuylercollection.tumblr.com/
- **Columbia University Archival Collections:** http://www.columbia.edu/cu/lweb/archival/collections/ldpd_4079745/

One last thing. This is the 3rd book in a series.

The *Arlington Playground Guide!!* is a review of all **70** playgrounds in Arlington, Virginia. We visited and reviewed all of them so you don't have to.

How Your City Works!! goes behind the scenes to show you all the activity (sewage, police, hospitals, recycling, animal shelters etc.) that males a city operate smoothly.

All these books are available in the Arlington, Virginia public library or on Amazon.com for **$10** each.

Made in the USA
Middletown, DE
06 June 2018